Bush Theatre

TENDER

by Eleanor Tindall

Tender was produced by Broccoli Arts and Jessie Anand Productions in association with the Bush Theatre and premiered at the Bush Theatre, London, on 19 November 2024.

TENDER

by Eleanor Tindall

Cast

Ivy	Nadi Kemp-Sayfi
Ash	Annabel Baldwin

Creative Team

Director	Emily Aboud
Set and Costume Designer	Alys Whitehead
Lighting Designer	David Doyle
Composer and Sound Designer	Ellie Isherwood
Intimacy Director	Tommy Ross-Williams
Production Manager	Chloe Stally-Gibson
Stage Manager	Nikita Bala
Producer	Broccoli Arts
Producer	Jessie Anand Productions

Supported by the Royal Victoria Hall Foundation

Cast

Nadi Kemp-Sayfi | Ivy

Nadi's theatre credits include *Julius Caesar*, *The Whip*, *A Museum in Baghdad* and *King John* (RSC); *Hakawatis*, *Women of the Arabian Nights*, *Much Ado About Nothing*, *As You Like It*, *Hansel and Gretel*, *The Tempest*, *Hamlet*, *Twelfth Night* and *A Midsummer Night's Dream* (Shakespeare's Globe); *Macbeth* (English Touring Theatre); *Macbeth: Something Wicked* (Donmar School Tour); *Repeat After Me*, *101 Dalmatians*, *Three Wheels on the Wagon*, *Between the Two*, *Homeland*, *The Witches' Promise* (Birmingham Repertory Theatre); *Bedroom Farce* (Queens Theatre, Hornchurch); *War with the News* (Knaive Theatre); *Burning Books*, *She* (Arena Theatre); *Wake* (Birmingham Opera Company); *Hijabi Monologues* (Bush Theatre); *Save Our School Dinners...Jamie!*, *Virilicus* (Belgrade Theatre Coventry); *Phone Home* (Upstart Theatre/ Creative Europe); *Comb*, *Aaron*, *Spiced Air* (RSC The Other Place); *Charity: To Give or Not to Give* (Birmingham MAC); *Little Stitches* (Time Won't Wait). Nadi's television appearances include *Eastenders* and *Charity Shop Sue* and radio includes *The Archers* and *Words and Music*.

Annabel Baldwin | Ash

Annabel's previous theatre appearances include *Harry Potter and the Cursed Child* where they originated the role of Moaning Myrtle (Palace Theatre); *Julius Caesar* (Royal Shakespeare Company); *The Wolves* (Theatre Royal Stratford East); *Wild Swimming* (Bristol Old Vic/Pleasance Theatre); *Antigone* (New Diorama Theatre); *Dear Elizabeth* (Gate Theatre); *Pride and Prejudice** (**sort of*) (Criterion Theatre); *How to Build a Wax Figure* (Pleasance Theatre).

Their television and film work includes *The Great* (Hulu); *Doctors* (BBC); *I Hate Suzie* (Amazon Prime); *The Jewish Enquirer* (Amazon Prime); *Love Wins* (Evolve Productions). Their audio work includes Anne Elliot in Audible's original adaptation of *Persuasion* and narrating novels including *Our Wives Under the Sea*, *Experienced* and *Faking It*.

Creative Team

Eleanor Tindall | Writer

Eleanor is a writer from London. Her debut play *Before I Was A Bear* premiered at The Bunker Theatre, gaining her a nomination for Best Writer at The Stage Debut Awards in 2020 and returning for a week to a sold-out audience at Soho Theatre in 2022. She has been a member of Soho Theatre Writers' Lab and taken part in writing workshops run by the Almeida and HighTide. Recently, Eleanor was commissioned by the Donmar Warehouse to adapt *Macbeth* for young audiences; her adaptation, *Macbeth: Something Wicked* toured schools across Camden and Westminster from June to July 2024 and reached over 3,500 young people. In 2024 Eleanor was selected as part of the BBC Voices programme and shortlisted for the Verity Bargate Award for her play *What If Orpheus Was Four Sad Women*.

Tender was a finalist for the 2023 Ambassador Theatre Group Playwright's Prize in association with Platform Presents.

Emily Aboud | Director

Emily Aboud is a Trinidadian theatre director. She was shortlisted for the 2023 RTST Sir Peter Hall Director Award and shortlisted for the JMK Director Award in 2022 and 2021. She is a recipient of the Evening Standard Future Theatre Fund Award. Recent credits include *Lady Dealer* (Bush Theatre/Paines Plough Roundabout); *Rock DJ and three other songs that saved the world* (New Diorama Theatre); *Haemosporidian* (Lyric Hammersmith); *Flip!* (Soho Theatre/regional tour); *Splintered* (which she also wrote) (Soho Theatre); *Close Quarters* (LAMDA); *Salt Slow* (RCSSD); *Bogeyman* (which she also wrote) (Edinburgh Fringe 2022) and *Pink Lemonade* (Bush Theatre). As a Caribbean theatre maker, her work draws inspiration from the political community theatre she grew up making in Trinidad – a combination of music, movement, direct audience address and theatricality.

Alys Whitehead | Set and Costume Designer

Alys Whitehead is a set and costume designer who trained at Central Saint Martins.

As designer, Alys' theatre work includes: *Bedroom Farce* (Queen's Theatre Hornchurch); *REVENGE: After the Levoyah* (Summerhall); *This Might Not Be It* (Bush Theatre); *The Angry Brigade* (LAMDA); *Sorry We Didn't Die At Sea*, *Snowflakes* (Park Theatre); *Lysistrata* (Lyric Hammersmith); *Sad* (Omnibus Theatre); *Maddie* (Arcola Theatre).

As associate designer, her work includes *Macbeth* (Harold Pinter Theatre); *The Glass

Menagerie (Rose Theatre/ Belgrade Theatre/ Alexandra Palace/UK Tour); *Earthworks* (Young Vic); *My Beautiful Laundrette* (Leicester Curve/UK tour); *Word-Play* (Royal Court); *Zoe's Peculiar Journey Through Time* (Theatre Rites/Southbank Centre/international tour); *Sea Creatures* (Hampstead Theatre).

Assistant designer credits include *Dixon and Daughters* (National Theatre).

David Doyle | Lighting Designer

David is a multi-award-winning lighting designer from Ireland.

Lighting work includes *Bellringers* (Hampstead Theatre/ Paines Plough Roundabout); *Bullring Techno Makeout Jamz* (Royal Court/Paines Plough Roundabout/UK tour); *we were promised honey!* (59E59/ Paines Plough Roundabout/ UK and international tour); *Life According to Saki* (New York Theatre Workshop/Edinburgh Fringe); *Instructions*, *Little Deaths* (Summerhall); *SAP* (Paines Plough Roundabout/ Soho Theatre/UK tour); *Nation* (Paines Plough Roundabout); *Boy in Da Korma* (Jermyn Street Theatre/Pleasance Theatre); *Fabulous Creatures*, *Anna Bella Eema* (Arcola Theatre); *Carmen*, *East*, *Outlying Islands* (King's Head Theatre); *The Last Show Before We Die* (Yard Theatre/ Bristol Old Vic/Paines Plough Roundabout); *Douze*, *The Power of Wow*, *Confirmation* (UK and Ireland tour); *ADMIN* (Project Arts Centre/Irish Tour); *Brendan Galileo For Europe* (Irish Tour); *Richard Carpenter is Close to You*, *My Name is Saoirse* (international tour).

David also works as a producer and is currently the Executive Producer for Jermyn Street Theatre.

Ellie Isherwood | Composer and Sound Designer

Ellie Isherwood is a sound designer, composer, actor/ musician and synth-pop artist (BYFYN). Her 'quietly groundbreaking' work spans a vast array of forms, from site-specific theatre to binaural audio experiences and musical theatre. Recent work includes composition and sound design for Fringe First Award-winning production, *Son of a Bitch* (Summerhall); *Rock DJ and three other songs that saved the world* (New Diorama Theatre) and *The Odyssey* (Unicorn Theatre).

Tommy Ross-Williams | Intimacy Director

Tommy Ross-Williams (they/ them) is a BECTU IC Registry Level 2 Intimacy Coordinator. They are also the Chair of the Intimacy Coordinators branch for BECTU. As an Intimacy Coordinator, Tommy has worked across stage and screen with BAFTA-nominated filmmakers, Turner Prize winners and Academy Award nominees.

Intimacy Direction credits include: *Brokeback Mountain*, *The Little Big Things* (@ sohoplace, West End); *Just for One Day* (Old Vic); *As You Like It* (Shakespeare's Globe); *Salty Irina* (Summerhall); *The Glass Menagerie* (Rose Theatre Kingston/UK tour).

Intimacy Coordination credits include: BBC, Disney, Amazon, Sky, BFI, Paramount, MTV, Universal Pictures, BFI and Apple TV. They are the Lead Intimacy Coordinator on the hit show *Sweetpea*, currently playing on Sky.

Tommy is also an award-winning writer/director. Recent credits include: *My Uncle Is Not Pablo Escobar* at Brixton House. As a screenwriter, they were selected for both BBC Writers: Voices 2024 programme and Climate Spring's Hot House Incubator.

Chloe Stally-Gibson | Production Manager

Chloe is a graduate of the Guildhall School of Music and Drama. She is an associate at Zoo Co Theatre Company and ChewBoy Productions. Chloe also works as the Deputy Production Manager at the Young Vic.

Her recent work includes: *Shifters* (Bush Theatre & Duke of York's Theatre); *Passing Strange*, *A Face In The Crowd* (Young Vic Theatre); *Perfect Show For Rachel* (Zoo Co/ Barbican); *This Might Not Be It* (Bush Theatre); *Silence* (Tara Theatre).

Nikita Bala | Stage Manager

Nikita Bala is a London-based freelance stage and production manager with a passion for all things technical. She has enjoyed collaborating on silly, clown-y shows, buzzing through festivals and touring across the country doing what she loves.

Past credits include *Nowhere* (Fuel Theatre), *Bangers* (Cardboard Citizens), *Lady Dealer* (Grace Dickson Productions), *Godot is a Woman* (Silent Faces Theatre), and *The Wolf, the Duck and the Mouse* (Unicorn Theatre).

Broccoli Arts | Producer

Broccoli Arts, a production company making work for/by/about lesbian, bisexual and queer people who experience misogyny, was founded by Salome Wagaine in 2019 and is now run by Eve Allin. Broccoli productions include *Tender*, *This Might Not Be It* (Bush Theatre); *Salty Irina* (Paines Plough Roundabout, Summerhall); *Before I Was a Bear* (Soho Theatre). Away from Broccoli, Eve Allin was Associate Producer at Soho Theatre for *Super High Resolution* and *Boys on the Verge of Tears*. Independently, she was producer for the internationally award-winning *Civilisation* by Jaz Woodcock-Stewart; *work.txt* by Nathan Ellis and *WRESTLELADSWRESTLE* by Jennifer Jackson. Eve is a Stage One supported producer.

Jessie Anand Productions | Producer

Jessie Anand Productions makes theatre and opera that is fresh and playful. Since it was founded in 2018, the company has premiered seven new plays: *This Might Not Be It* (Bush Theatre); *Tiger* (Omnibus Theatre); *Orlando* (59E59, New York/Pleasance Theatre, Edinburgh/VAULT Festival); *Pennyroyal* (Finborough Theatre); *Yellowfin* (Southwark Playhouse); *MAGDALENE* (Arcola Theatre) and *Blue Thunder* (VAULT Festival). Other productions include the national premieres of Angus Cerini's Griffin Award-winning play *The Bleeding Tree* (Southwark Playhouse) and Amy Beach's 1932 opera *Cabildo* (Wilton's Music Hall/Arcola Theatre). Jessie Anand Productions also develops new musical theatre and is currently working on Maz O'Connor's new musical *The Wife of Michael Cleary*, which won the MTI Stiles and Drewe Mentorship Award. Jessie Anand Productions is thirteen times Offie-nominated and supported by Stage One.

Bush Theatre

We make theatre for London. Now.

For over 50 years the Bush Theatre has been a world-famous home for new plays and an internationally renowned champion of playwrights.

Combining ambitious artistic programming with meaningful community engagement work and industry leading talent development schemes, the Bush Theatre champions and supports unheard voices to develop the artists and audiences of the future.

Since opening in 1972 the Bush has produced more than 500 ground-breaking premieres of new plays, developing an enviable reputation for its acclaimed productions nationally and internationally.

They have nurtured the careers of writers including James Graham, Lucy Kirkwood, Temi Wilkey, Jonathan Harvey and Jack Thorne. Recent successes include Tyrell Williams' *Red Pitch*, Benedict Lombe's *Shifters*, and Arinzé Kene's *Misty*. The Bush has won over 100 awards including the Olivier Award for Outstanding Achievement in Affliate Theatre for the past four years for Richard Gadd's *Baby Reindeer*, Igor Memic's *Old Bridge*, Waleed Akhtar's *The P Word* and Matilda Feyiṣayọ Ibini's *Sleepova*.

Located in the renovated old library on Uxbridge Road in the heart of Shepherd's Bush, the Bush Theatre continues to create a space where all communities can be part of its future and call the theatre home.

'The place to go for ground-breaking work as diverse as its audiences' EVENING STANDARD

bushtheatre.co.uk
@bushtheatre

h&f hammersmith & fulham

Supported by ARTS COUNCIL ENGLAND

Artistic Director	Lynette Linton
Executive Director	Mimi Findlay
Associate Artistic Director	Daniel Bailey
Deputy Executive Director	Angela Wachner
Development & Marketing Assistant	Nicima Abdi
Development Officer	Laura Aiton
Head of Marketing	Shannon Clarke
Head of Development	Jocelyn Cox
Associate Dramaturg	Titilola Dawudu
Finance Assistant	Lauren Francis
Resident Director & Young Company Director	Katie Greenall
Technical & Buildings Manager	Jamie Haigh
Assistant Venue Manager	Rae Harm
Head of Finance	Neil Harris
Marketing Officer	Laela Henley-Rowe
Associate Producer	Nikita Karia
Community Assistant	Joanne Leung
Senior Producer	Oscar Owen
Assistant Venue Manager	Simon Pilling
Senior Technician	John Pullig
Event Sales Manager & Technician	Charlie Sadler
Venue Manager (Theatre)	Ade Seriki
Press Manager	Martin Shippen
Community Producer	Holly Smith
Literary & Producing Assistant	Laetitia Somè
Marketing Manager	Ed Theakston
Assistant Venue Manager (Box Office)	Robin Wilks
Theatre Administrator & Executive Assistant	Chloe Wilson
Café Bar Manager	Wayne Wilson

DUTY MANAGERS
Sara Dawood, Molly Elson, Thomas Ingram, Madeleine Simpson-Kent & Anna-May Wood.

VENUE SUPERVISORS
Antony Baker, Addy Caulder-James, Stephanie Cremona, Emma Chatel, Zea Hilland, Nzuzi Malemda, Roy Mas, Jacob Meier & Louis Nicholson.

VENUE ASSISTANTS
Javine Aduganfi, Doridan Bavangila, Charlotte Binns, Will Byam-Shaw, Pyerre Clarke, Daniel Fesoom, Matias Hailu, Bo Leandro, Maya Li Preti, Ishani McGuire, Khy Matinez, April Miller, Ed Mendoza, Carys Murray, Chana Nardone, Jennifer Okolo, James Robertson, Ali Shah & Nefertari Williams.

Bush Theatre, 7 Uxbridge Road, London W12 8LJ
Box Office: 020 8743 5050 | Administration: 020 8743 3584
Email: info@bushtheatre.co.uk | bushtheatre.co.uk

THANK YOU

Our supporters make our work possible. Together, we're evolving the canon and creating a bolder, more diverse, and representative future for British theatre. We're so grateful to you all.

MAJOR DONORS
Charles Holloway OBE
Jim & Michelle Gibson
Georgia Oetker
Cathy & Tim Score
Susie Simkins
Jack Thorne
Gianni & Michael Alen-Buckley

SHOOTING STARS
Jim & Michelle Gibson
Cathy & Tim Score
Susie Simkins

LONE STARS
Jax & Julian Bull
Clyde Cooper
Adam Kenwright
Anthony Marraccino & Mariela Manso
Jim Marshall
Georgia Oetker

HANDFUL OF STARS
Charlie Bigham
Judy Bollinger
David des Jardins
Sue Fletcher
Thea Guest
Elizabeth Jack
Simon & Katherine Johnson
Joanna Kennedy
Garry & Lorna Lawrence
Phyllida Lloyd & Kate Pakenham
Vivienne Lukey
Aditya Mittal
Sam & Jim Murgatroyd
Mark & Anne Paterson
Martha Plimpton
Nick & Annie Reid
Bhagat Sharma
Joe Tinston & Amelia Knott
Dame Emma Thompson

RISING STARS
Elizabeth Beebe
Martin Blackburn
David Brooks
Catharine Browne
Anthony Chantry
Lauren Clancy
Richard & Sarah Clarke
Caroline Clasen
Susan Cuff
Matthew Cushen
Anne-Hélène and Rafaël Biosse Duplan
Austin Erwin
Kim Evans
Mimi Findlay
Jack Gordon
Hugh & Sarah Grootenhuis
Sarah Harrison
Uzma Hasan
Lesley Hill & Russ Shaw
Davina & Malcolm Judelson
Mike Lewis
Lynette Linton
Michael McCoy
Judy Mellor
Caro Millington
Rajiv Nathwani
Yoana Nenova
Stephen Pidcock
Miguel & Valeri Ramos Handal
Karen & John Seal
James St. Ville KC
Jan Topham
Kit & Anthony van Tulleken
Evanna White
Ben Yeoh

CORPORATE SPONSORS
Biznography
Casting Pictures Ltd.
Nick Hern Books
S&P Global
The Agency

TRUSTS & FOUNDATIONS
Backstage Trust
Buffini Chao Foundation
Christina Smith Foundation
Daisy Trust
Esmée Fairbairn Foundation
The Foyle Foundation
Garfield Weston Foundation
Garrick Charitable Trust
Hammersmith United Charities
The Harold Hyam Wingate Foundation
Idlewild Trust
Jerwood Foundation
Martin Bowley Charitable Trust
Noël Coward Foundation
The Thistle Trust

And all the donors who wish to remain anonymous.

If you are interested in finding out how to be involved, please visit **bushtheatre.co.uk/support-us** email **development@bushtheatre.co.uk** or call **020 8743 3584**.

TENDER

Eleanor Tindall

Acknowledgements

From the bottom of my heart, thank you to:

My mum and dad, Hannah Dunne, Oscar Owen, Eve Allin, Emily Aboud, Jessie Anand, Alys Whitehead, Chloe Stally-Gibson, Ellie Isherwood, David Doyle, Nikita Bala, Nadi Kemp-Sayfi, Annabel Baldwin, Tommy Ross-Williams, Shannon Clarke, Aneesha Srinivasan, Mariella Johnson, Kara Fitzpatrick, Nikita Karia, Titilola Dawudu, Lynette Linton, Daniel Bailey, Deborah Halsey, Maddie Hindes, Polina Kalinina, Josh Cockroft and everyone at the Bush Theatre.

E.T.

tender / "tɛndə" [*adjective*]
gentle / painful / soft

Give wine. Give bread. Give back your heart
to itself, to the stranger who has loved you
all your life

Derek Walcott, 'Love After Love'

Characters

ASH, *woman*
IVY, *woman*
CAS, *man*
MAX, *man*

Note on Casting

This was written for a cast of two, with the actor playing Ash also playing Max and Cas, but it could also be done with a cast of three/four.

Note on the Text

A forward slash (/) indicates an interruption in speech.

Three asterisks (***) indicates a shift in time and/or space.

An asterisk (*) indicates words that should be spoken simultaneously (or as close to simultaneously as possible).

Sometimes Ash and Ivy speak to us when they are also in dialogue with another character (or each other). This is marked in square brackets [like this].

Words in (round brackets) do not have to be spoken, they are there to show intention – do whatever feels right.

There is music throughout, indicated in italics within square brackets [*like this*]. These songs are not set in stone and should be seen more as a guide if licensing does not allow their use.

This text went to press before the end of rehearsals and so may differ slightly from the play as performed.

A pulsating yellow wall.

IVY*'s hands are covered in blood.* ASH *has a rucksack on her back. She looks extremely tired.*

IVY I'm sixteen and I've decided to cut parts of myself out and hide them in the walls of my bedroom
It feels like the only option
It isn't hard – I just reach down inside my throat, push through my body and grab, or push my fingers through my skin and rip things out that way instead
Pull at whatever I can find, whatever I can find that's fighting, pulsing, shouting
I tear down the wall and place the parts in there one by one
Then put the walls back together one by one
Bricks and mortar come to me out of nowhere and the room swallows me up gratefully, hungrily –

ASH Can you hear that?

The estate agent's looking at me, puzzled – Hear what? He says, pacing around the room, each of his movements fanning a wave of aftershave in my direction –

They cough.

He listens for a second before telling me he's got to go because he has another viewing sweetheart, and do I want it or not sweetheart?? Cos if I don't take it now it'll be gone sweetheart!! So cheap and so close to the station he's got queues of people wanting this place – virtual queues sweetheart! He assures me as I turn to look out of the window –

Heartbeat.

ASH *listens.*

It's in a house that's been gutted and split
Three rooms – a kitchen-cum-living room-cum-everything else, tiny bathroom, hallway, bedroom
He's impatient – his polished grin pulls at the edges of his mouth so I apologise and I take it because it *is* cheap and it *is* close to the station, and I'm desperate and estate agents have an instinct for desperation
It's got a smell, it's hard to cover up and estate agents – they sniff it out like dogs and they go for you
He has definitely gone for me
I sort of welcome it in a weird way, the feeling of his teeth hooked into my skin

ASH *throws her bag onto the floor.* IVY *winces.* ASH *hears but doesn't know where it's coming from.* IVY *starts to clean her hands.* ASH *changes clothes.*

IVY We move out

Finally I can leave them here, leave them behind
I don't need them anyway all they do is cause trouble
They cry when we go, huge gurgling repulsive howls
I can still hear them as the removal van lurches down our street
Onto the main road
Nearly
Left –

IVY *exhales. Dries her hands.*

ASH *goes to the wall. Puts her ear up against it.*

No one can see the holes in my body
I've hidden them
It's like a magic trick

ASH There is something about this house
It's loud with something

I don't mind too much because I don't like silence
In silence I just look for things that aren't there –

IVY *sneezes.* ASH *turns sharply. Stares.*

I'm not used to having so much space just for me
I walk around naked and I piss with the door open, shit with the door open, eat with my mouth open
Sauce all over my face like a baby

I watch problematic TV shows that I shouldn't like and I play the same song again and again

I can almost convince myself that this is how it's always been
As if nothing came before this
As if there was no other me before this

Heartbeats.

IVY You might say that my life is perfect

I have a boyfriend and a flat and everything is in place, I can see how my life will pan out, I could draw a map of my life if you asked me to
It's a relief to know I am in the right place

Heartbeats, louder and faster. ASH *goes to the wall. Listens.* IVY *fidgets.*

ASH *hits the wall very hard. Winces.*

The heartbeat slows.

[*'Lonely Day' – System of a Down.*]

ASH I've been to this night a few times
A lot actually, since I moved
The first time I drank a whole bottle of wine before I even got there which was probably a mistake, definitely a mistake actually but I'm better at it now – mostly

ASH *walks.*

IVY Max is away working for the night so I have the flat to myself

I open my mouth and swallow his absence, feel it fill me up

IVY *inhales.*

I stare at the early evening blue sky outside and feel hungry for it, for the feeling of the low sun on my skin
I go for a walk

IVY *puts shoes on. Finds a packet of tobacco.*

I don't actually smoke. I've given up, so it's fine for me to buy a packet every now and then, because I've technically quit. This isn't proper smoking. I bought this ages ago just for emergencies, or when I'm stressed or angry or drinking, or like, with friends or on holiday

IVY *opens the packet, inhales hungrily, eyes closed. Rolls a cigarette. Walks.*

ASH I do kind of wish I'd had a drink before I left
Not a whole bottle of wine, just something little
I think about buying a can for the train and then remember I'm thirty years of age –

IVY *searches for a lighter, can't find one.*

I guess I could get a can and decant it into a water bottle? Then at least no one will judge me, apart from myself –

IVY Sorry, excuse me, have you got a light?

The music stops.

Blood spurts out of IVY*, straight onto* ASH*'s shoes.* ASH *jumps.* IVY *doesn't react.*

ASH Oh my / god!!

IVY Whoa, sorry

ASH Fuck

IVY Sorry I'll ask someone / else

ASH Are you okay?!

IVY Yeah are you?!

ASH Really?

IVY Yeah?!

ASH Are you / sure?

IVY Yeah / why

ASH Do you want me to get someone??

IVY Get – what? What for?

ASH *looks behind her. Looks back at* IVY. *Stares at her for a moment.*

Heartbeat.

ASH Sorry, I just –

IVY What?

ASH ? – Nothing

IVY ?

ASH Honestly nothing

IVY Okay – do you have a / lighter or

ASH Lighter, sorry – hold on

ASH *looks through her pockets.*

It's here somewhere

IVY I can ask someone / else

ASH Got it

IVY *lights her cigarette.*

Sorry about that

IVY *hands the lighter back.*

IVY Thanks

ASH No worries

IVY *walks away.*

Hallucination
Trick of the light
Or something

ASH *walks.*

I get on the Tube and I bite my nails
There's a woman sitting opposite me, her little kid is playing with a snake toy
He runs around the carriage
Sees me looking and hisses shyly
I play along
The woman shoots me a tired smile and he sinks his teeth into her arm when she isn't looking
When he pulls away there's a tiny bit of blood on his lip
I get to the bar and stop biting my nails because I remember someone once told me it was a form of cannibalism plus it's not a very good look so I sit down and try to drink in the mood lighting and I feel everything slow down a bit, at last, and I order a pint and I look down at my shoes and realise they're still covered in blood –

Heartbeats

The air is going a bit too fast past me and I wonder if I'm having some kind of stroke or haemorrhage and I laugh cos I imagine the police turning up at my parent's house and telling them that I'd died at a club night called Aphrodyki –

ASH*'s pint appears. She downs half of it.*

A bottle of wine appears. IVY *opens it. Pours a glass. Drinks.*

IVY I wonder where she was going? The woman with the lighter. She looked casual but the jacket made me think she was going *out* out somewhere, a bar maybe, to meet some friends or maybe she was going on a date

ASH I spot this group
There's a woman in a blue crop top with bleached blonde hair and orange lipstick

She looks up, smiles at me
Looks at me for a bit too long
Then looks back at her phone
I wait a minute, take another sip of beer
Feel a bit softer and braver already
I catch her looking again, catch her eyeing me up and down
Not very subtle
I start to forget about the woman I saw
About her blood on my shoes

IVY I think about what it would be like to be in Soho on a warm night like this
So many people you can't hear yourself think

I wonder if she got on the Tube, what stop she got off at –

ASH We go back to mine
Her name's Sara and she works at a law firm and we talk about music and TV and the state of the government and I am deft in avoiding any questions about family
It's always a dodgy one
You never know which way it's going to go and she doesn't press
She's a bit older than me and I'm drunker than her but not sloppy drunk, just drunk enough that everything feels easy
I love this feeling
I feel brand new
Like nothing came before

Heartbeats. ASH *tries to ignore it.*

IVY I imagine that I'm in a smoking area, crushed against people
Maybe the woman with the lighter is there

Drinks.

[*'Cry to Me' – Solomon Burke.*]

IVY dances, drinks. She might have another cigarette. Heartbeats.

ASH We have sex

It's good

Heartbeats, faster.

It's good

Heartbeats, faster.

I start to get a bit distracted because the walls won't
Stop
Fucking
Thumping
I can't take my eyes off this bit of the wall where the wallpaper is uneven
It doesn't quite match up
The pattern doesn't flow properly
It starts to go one way then it skips
Someone's put it together wrong –
Why the fuck would you do that?? How could you be so stupid?
I try and look away and see my shoes in the corner of the room, blood crusting around the soles and
I feel like my stomach is about to come out of my mouth –

Blood spurts out of IVY.

I stop
Make my excuses – sorry, a bit too drunk, my antidepressants
She is unfazed, kisses me on the cheek
She leaves

They exhale.

***

ASH Sorry, are you / open?

IVY Jesus / fuck!

ASH Oh – sorry!

IVY Scared the shit out of / me

ASH I'm really sorry, I sort of knew that was going to happen but I didn't know how to avoid / it

IVY We're not open yet

ASH Ah okay – door was (open) so I just / assumed

IVY Yeah, I must've forgotten to shut it

ASH No worries

IVY My fault

ASH I'll – thanks anyway

ASH *goes to leave. Stops.*

Is it you?

IVY What?

ASH Did I lend you a lighter yesterday?

IVY Oh, yeah

ASH I – yeah

IVY Thanks for that

ASH No worries!

Beat.

IVY Do you want a coffee?

ASH I'm – fine I think I'll go to the Costa by the / station

IVY It's closed. Fight or something, windows were smashed

ASH Ah

IVY What would you like?

ASH You're not open / yet

IVY It's fine just, would you like one or not?

ASH Okay, yeah. If you don't / mind

IVY Cappuccino, latte, Americano, flat / white

ASH Flat white please

IVY *starts making* ASH *a coffee.*

Thanks

IVY Regular milk?

ASH Oat, if you have it

IVY *nods.*

IVY Did you want a pastry?

ASH Have you got any almond croissants?

IVY *nods.* ASH *watches her as she makes the coffee.*

IVY *passes* ASH *her flat white and the pastry. She inspects it. Takes the lid off the coffee, inspects that too. Takes a sip.*

ASH Mmm thanks, how much?

IVY Eight pound seventy-five.

ASH Wow

IVY Yeah

ASH Okay

ASH *gets out her card. Pays.*

Can I have a loyalty card?

IVY Sure

ASH Thanks

IVY *gets a loyalty card, stamps it once. Then twice.*

Oh haha, thanks.

IVY *gives it to* ASH.

I hope your day is good

IVY You too. I hope your day is good too.

Beat.

I like your jacket

ASH Oh! Cheers.

Beat.

IVY Bye

ASH (*Waves loyalty card.*) See you tomorrow?

IVY Okay!

ASH Yeah!

IVY Bye

ASH Bye

IVY Bye bye

ASH *leaves. Blood spurts out of* IVY. *She exhales, winces.*

***

IVY I get home from work and Max isn't back yet

I've had this feeling all day like I could fuck anything that moves
It's blistering
I must be about to come on

Guilty –

I go and get my laptop

I know it's bad to watch porn and I don't watch it regularly it's just every now and then and also this site is apparently very ethical and made by women –

Heartbeats.

ASH *stares at the wall. Goes over to it. Touches it gently.* IVY *quivers.*

ASH *puts her ear and both hands up against the wall. Listens. Traces her hands over it.*

IVY *sighs.*

Her phone rings.

My brother calls me
Right in the middle
I ignore it
He calls again

I ignore it
He calls again –

IVY *answers her phone.*

Hi Cas can I ring you / back?

CAS What you doing?

IVY I can't talk right / now

CAS Why?

IVY Because I'm busy

CAS You still at work?

IVY I – yes

CAS [*As if he's on the edge of tears.*] I'm just having a really bad day

IVY *inhales. Exhales.*

IVY I'm sorry to hear / that

CAS Can I meet you?

IVY When?

CAS Well now ideally. I need you Ivy

IVY I can't right / now

CAS End of the week then. Thursday?

IVY Okay, will have to be after work / though

CAS Is Max around?

IVY He will be

CAS Sick

IVY See you then

CAS You annoyed with me?

IVY No

CAS You said I could ring anytime

IVY Yes I / know

CAS So I'm doing that

IVY Good. That's good

IVY *inhales, exhales.*

As soon as I put the phone down Max gets home –

MAX There she / is!

IVY Thought you weren't back till nine!

MAX I got a lift with Stefan – give me a kiss!! You okay?

IVY Yeah tired, long day

[He comes into the bedroom and sweeps me into a hug and a kiss on the cheek
His face is bristly and he smells of outside air and mint and petrol]

You need a shave

[His hands are on my bare legs]

MAX So do you!!

IVY Dick

MAX Oh so I'm not allowed to say it to / you?!

IVY No

MAX Doesn't sound like equality / to me, babe

IVY Please

MAX Oi! I'm obviously joking, also I don't care they're just prickly. Like a porcupine

IVY A porcupine

[Hands further up my bare legs]

MAX Yes. I missed you. You look good.

IVY Do I

MAX Yes you do. A sexy porcupine

IVY I'm hungry shall we have some dinner? Maybe we could go to the pub get a burger or / something

MAX Come lie with / me

IVY Also Cas called, wants to see us Thursday

MAX Oh great, that'll be a barrel of laughs

IVY Don't be mean

MAX I'm not he's just haaaard / work at the moment

IVY Well he's been through a lot

MAX He's always going through things isn't he

IVY I can't have this conversation / right now

MAX Come / hereeee

IVY Nah I'm hungry I wanna eat

MAX Wait – what's that?

IVY What?

[Hands on my bare legs, I stare at the laptop really really hard, try and get it to disappear, or burst into flames, or sink into the ground but it doesn't and neither do I unfortunately]

MAX Are you watching porn?

IVY No that's not – that's not porn

MAX Can't believe you started without / me

IVY No it's just an – erm, a French film. Arthouse film.

MAX A pornographic French arthouse / film

IVY I wasn't like, watching it watching it, not seriously watching it

MAX Sure. Just background noise?

IVY Yeah?

MAX Yeah nice try but I was a teenage boy once and I do know all the excuses, unfortunately

IVY Can we just go for dinner and forget this ever happened

MAX Didn't know you were into girl on girl. That's hot

IVY Let's go, please –

***

ASH *sits.*

ASH I finish work early but I'm a bit restless so I take the long way home and go to the park
It's warm, unnervingly warm for late September –
Claustrophobic, makes my skin feel tight
I buy a can of coke and find a bench
Go to scroll and then remember –
I text Sara apologising for the other night and we message for a bit but it's really mundane and boring so I stop replying after a while
I'm not ghosting
I don't owe her anything.
'You Don't Owe Anyone Anything.' I saw that on Instagram, an activist, well, influencer I know made it into a print so it must be true

Heartbeats.

Suddenly there is this
Prickling on the back of my neck
Like someone is watching me
Like someone is about to –

ASH*'s phone rings. She stares at it. It stops. It rings again.*

He'll get bored after a while and give up.

Phone rings again.

He'll get bored after a while and

ASH *shifts uncomfortably.*

Text alert. ASH *opens it. Heartbeats.*

ASH *stands bolt upright and walks.*

IVY Max persuades me after a while
Asks so many times I feel bad
I don't want to hurt his feelings
And I am – I was close to –
Maybe I want to now, now he's asked so much
Now he's touched me so much, maybe now I want to Just let him get on with it
Just let myself be swallowed whole

ASH I take a different route out of the park
Get to the main road
Try to stop shaking
There's a church opposite with people dressed up outside
Big shiny cars
Come on
Surely not
I pray that it's a funeral
Please be a funeral
Please be a funeral

The doors open and I see a flash of white

Heartbeats.

MAX You okay in there?!

IVY Fine sorry just, don't feel well

MAX Wasn't that bad was it / haha

IVY No just give me a minute

MAX Hurry up I need a piss

IVY One sec –

***

ASH I go into a pub bathroom
Check my phone and delete the text
It was probably just to scare me
He couldn't really see me
He couldn't *actually* see me he just said it to freak me out, surely
I can still feel that prickling on the back of my neck it's like a rash like a burn –
I order an Uber and focus on the little car icon, watch as it moves closer and closer to the little pin icon, then I thank the girl behind the bar as I come out, say something about being unwell, she looks mildly disgusted at the thought of having to clean up any mess that I might have made which is fair and I feel a bit guilty but then I realise that I haven't

actually left any mess for her to clean up and for fuck's sake everyone should be allowed to use the toilet shouldn't they? Isn't it a human right? The Uber arrives, interrupting the argument I've started to have with myself about toilet access and I leave the pub and get in the car –

ASH *exhales.*

I get home

ASH *puts her hand on the wall.*

The noise of the flat is welcoming this time I want it to eat me up, fill me up –

ASH *finds the corner of the wall where the paper is coming away. She very gently tries to peel it.*

I can't stop thinking about the girl from the café
Her face is so clear in my mind
I close my eyes and I can see hers
Hot and piercing –
The hairs on her arm
The gold ring on her thumb
Her neck as she turned – her hair trailing down to that bit, that bit where the sun was hitting
That bit just under her ear –

ASH *pulls harder at the wall –* IVY *audibly winces.*

ASH *stops. Strokes the wall. Leans against it.* IVY *sighs.*

ASH *sighs.*

They sleep.

***

IVY I wake up at seven a.m. with a tight chest

Max is still asleep and his arm is flung over me
It's so heavy, like rock, and I have to really shove it to get it off

He murmurs in protest, rolls towards me
He's bigger than last night, taller, and his skin is cold and hard
I kiss him on his forehead
When I pull away I feel like there's grit all over my chin –

IVY *brushes her face. Looks at her hand.*

I go into the bathroom expecting to find my period but nothing yet
I get ready
Open the door –

IVY *hungrily gasps for air.*

***

ASH *eats a pain au chocolat.* IVY *makes her a coffee.*

ASH So good

IVY Buttery

ASH So buttery

IVY Perfect amount of chocolate

ASH Yeah

They eat.

IVY Where do you work then?

ASH Ealing

IVY West!

ASH Yeah

IVY Bit of a trek!

ASH From here / yeah

IVY That's *West* West as well, must take you hours!

ASH One / hour

IVY What do you do?

ASH Just admin at a clinic

IVY How comes you live here if you work in *West*?

ASH Why do you say West like it's a swear word?

IVY Just far, isn't it?

ASH I lived there years ago. Then I moved away for a bit, then I came back and the job was there again

IVY Lucky

ASH Mm

IVY Where did you move to?

ASH Spain

IVY Wow! How comes?

ASH Just, existential crisis, I dunno

IVY Oh jeez

ASH No not really I just felt a bit lost I think, wanted something new

IVY So you moved country

ASH Where do you live?

IVY Round the corner, near the Victoria

ASH Oh nice

IVY *hands* ASH *her coffee.*

Thanks.

Sips.

IVY How come you left Spain?

ASH Didn't suit me, didn't work

IVY Good food though

ASH Yeah lots of / tapas

IVY Paella, oh yeah, tapas. And the weather

ASH You live with friends? Or?

IVY Boyfriend

ASH Oh wow, that's great

IVY Yeah it's great

ASH Great

IVY You live with friends? Boyfriend?

ASH Ha, no I live alone

IVY Oh wow. Grown up

ASH I guess

IVY Your own space

ASH Yeah it's great

IVY Great.

ASH How long have you been with your boyfriend?

IVY Four years

ASH Long / time

IVY Do you speak any Spanish then?

ASH Erm

IVY You must speak some if you used to live there

ASH Un poco

IVY Is that it?

ASH What's his name?

IVY Who?

ASH Your boyfriend

IVY Max, why?

ASH Just curious

IVY You got a boyfriend?

ASH No. I don't really date boys much

IVY Oh okay

ASH Well, men. Any more

ASH *turns to look out of the window.*

IVY How come?

ASH How come?

IVY Yeah?

ASH That's a weird question

IVY Is it? Sorry

ASH No It's fine.

I dunno.
I always knew I'd stop at one point, I think

Blood spurts out of IVY.

***

ASH I'm on the Tube home from work listening to a podcast
Keep having to rewind it because I'm not really paying attention
I gaze sleepily into the next carriage and
Out of the corner of my eye I swear I see –
I can't be sure
Someone's stood right in front of him
If he would just turn
If he would just turn
Ever
So
Slightly –

IVY No one's home when I get back

IVY *exhales.*

I send a text to my brother asking when he'll be here

IVY *eats everything in sight. A glass of water appears. She drinks half of it fast. Spills on herself maybe. Puts the glass down. Pauses.*

A thumping noise that gets closer and closer. IVY *eyes the glass of water as it ripples.*

ASH I get off the Tube and walk very quickly onto a bus
I sit right at the back in the corner

IVY My brother arrives smelling of meat –

A slab of venison.

Why did you bring that?

CAS They were giving them away to staff

IVY What even is it?

CAS Deer

IVY Eurgh

CAS It's venison, it's fucking posh, don't be ungrateful

IVY I'm a / vegetarian

MAX She's a vegetarian Cas you do know that

IVY Put it in the fridge then so I can't see / it

CAS 'Vegetarian'

IVY Want a drink?

CAS (*Clicking.*) Cold beers asap sis

[*'Glory Box' – Portishead.*]

***

ASH I get home and –

A bunch of yellow lilies.

ASH *inhales. Coughs. Retches. Reads the note. Shoves it in her mouth. Spits it out. Goes to stamp on the lilies.*

Stops.

***

IVY Explain again

MAX I've just / *said*

IVY Explain again

MAX I just think that there must've been something really wrong for her to do / that

IVY Okay so why didn't she just say?

MAX Maybe she did

IVY She didn't. Cas did she ever speak to you about feeling / unhappy?

CAS I don't / know

IVY See

MAX He said he didn't know that's not a no is / it

IVY Whose side are you on?

MAX I'm on Cas's side obviously but I don't think this, this way of doing things is really going to get you anywhere mate

IVY What else is he supposed to do if she won't answer his / calls?

CAS Yeah, no other way seems to work

IVY *drinks.*

IVY She's a bitch

MAX I think we're all agreed on that I / just

IVY You just said, you just basically blamed my brother / for it

MAX I really didn't

IVY I hate her

MAX You never even met her

IVY I don't need to hate her to know, I don't – I don't need to know her to know, to know that I hate / her

MAX Alright. I think you've had too much to drink

IVY Whatever

CAS She humiliated me in front of my / entire family, Maxy

IVY Family, friends, everyone

MAX I agree with you! We are all agreeing with each other! We're just drunk so we're shouting about / it

IVY Give me her Instagram

MAX Jesus Christ, Ivy she deleted it. Cas has said this roughly eight times tonight you should have some water

IVY I'm / fine

CAS Jeez. You two gonna bicker like this when you have kids

IVY Shut up Cas

CAS Pressure will be back on you now the wedding's / off

IVY I'm gonna get some more / wine

CAS What's taking you so long anyway! Weak swimmers is it Maxy?

IVY *goes into the kitchen. The big slab of venison is there, glistening.*

She stares. Licks her lips. IVY *picks up the venison and eats it raw with her hands.*

When she is done she pulls out a box of ice cream from the freezer and eats it straight from the tub.

***

MAX I put him in an Uber

IVY Want some ice cream?

MAX No thanks that's – been there for a while

Beat.

Well. That was an interesting evening

IVY Mmm

MAX I worry about him sometimes

IVY Yeah.

Beat.

He's so heartbroken

MAX No I mean. I worry about what he'll do

IVY What do you mean?

***

ASH I try to calm down
Put on a BBC crime drama and pour myself a glass of wine
Drink it fast
Pour another
The drama isn't very good but I can't seem to stop and before I know it I've watched five episodes
Also Nicola Walker is in it and there is something so comforting about her
I watch her ponder the murder of a woman over a yellow Styrofoam box of chips and I suddenly realise I forgot to eat dinner
I consider cooking something but my hands won't stop shaking
Empty stomach
Nerves shot
Dehydrated –
So I order a takeaway

Beat.

Phone rings.

I assume that the driver's got lost –

Answers.

Hello?

Inhales.

Cas? Cas.
I know it's you

Heartbeats.

Leave me alone
Leave me the fuck alone

Hangs up.

***

IVY He's harmless

MAX He's not *harmless* though is he babe

IVY What do you mean?

MAX You know what I / mean

IVY No I don't wanna go into any of that I've had too much to drink

MAX Sorry, but he's got / form

IVY I just said to leave it. Please.

Heartbeats.

MAX Sorry. Hey.

I'm sorry.

I didn't mean to – I just. I hate the thought of it

It makes my heart hurt

Beat.

Anyway. Can you believe what he said about my sperm?

IVY Your sperm?

MAX 'Weak swimmers is it / Maxy'

IVY Oh

MAX I fucking *hate* when he calls me Maxy

IVY Tell him not to / then

MAX I have millions of times, you know I have

IVY *yawns.*

Do you think I have weak swimmers?

IVY I've never really thought about / it

MAX I think my swimmers are like fucking Arnold Schwarzenegger

IVY I'm sure they / are

MAX Terminator sperm!!

Beat.

IVY I think I'm gonna go to bed

MAX Sorry haha

IVY No, I'm just so tired

MAX I'm gonna have a shower

IVY Okay

MAX Want to come?

IVY Not really

MAX Why?

IVY Don't fancy it

MAX Don't fancy me?

IVY No just don't fancy *it*. Tired, drank a bit too much, feel a bit / sick

MAX Would it help if I put some lesbian porn on?

IVY Fuck off

MAX I'm joking, come on it'll be fun

IVY I'm not in the mood

MAX We used to fuck in the shower all the time

IVY I'm *tired* Max

MAX Okay okay

Beat.

I'll be thinking about you though. You in that black dress you wore to the wedding

IVY It isn't really a wedding if the bride doesn't turn / up

MAX You looked so fucking / hot

IVY Why did I wear black to a wedding actually. That's meant to be bad luck isn't it

MAX Come kiss me –

IVY Maybe I caused it, maybe I'm the reason she didn't come – do you think he blames me? Do you think I cursed it? Is it my fault?

MAX Ivy.

Come with me –

IVY [I go upstairs with him

I tell him again that I don't fancy it and he leaves looking wounded]

Later he comes to bed, wet from the shower, like a cold mossy rock and he runs his gravelly hands all over my body, says he just wants to touch me a bit
Can he just touch me a bit?
So I let him
So he does –

***

The café. IVY *is struggling with a table.* ASH *is drinking coffee.*

ASH It's gonna drop

IVY It's not

ASH Just let me help

IVY No, I'm good thank you

ASH I don't think you / are

IVY I'm / fine

ASH You're gonna – I think it's gonna / fall

IVY It's not –

ASH *runs over to stop the table from falling.*

ASH Got it

IVY Left

They move left. Put the table down. They are suddenly aware that they are very close to each other. They move away.

Thanks

ASH Sure

IVY I did have it

ASH Course you / did

IVY Just tired

ASH What did you do last night?

IVY Saw my brother

ASH Fun?

IVY No

ASH No?

IVY Not fun

ASH You don't get on?

IVY No we do, I love my brother

ASH Okay

IVY You going out tonight?

ASH Why?

IVY Dunno, Friday isn't it. Most people go out on a Friday

ASH Most people don't work Saturdays

IVY I do

ASH I hate working Saturdays cos of the mob

IVY / Mob?

ASH / Wait are you going out then?

IVY Nah

ASH Might go to the pub

IVY Nice

ASH Wanna come?

IVY Me?

ASH No, the coffee machine

IVY I dunno

ASH You don't have to

IVY I should see what Max is doing

ASH Bring him if you want

IVY You just going on your own?

ASH If you're not coming then yeah

IVY *tilts her head.*

What?

IVY Isn't that a bit

ASH A bit what?

IVY Like – isn't it a bit sad

Ash ?

IVY I'm not being rude

ASH You are a bit, but that's / fine

IVY I'm not I / just think

ASH You don't like doing things on your own?

IVY No I like it sometimes

ASH Why does it bother you / then?

IVY It doesn't *bother me* but don't you worry what people will think?

ASH No I don't really care what people think

IVY I don't believe anyone who says that

ASH Well. Maybe that's a you problem

Beat.

IVY Are you offended

ASH No, I just think it's a bit judgemental

IVY Sorry.

ASH Have you never gone out for a meal or a drink on your own? Ever?

IVY No, why would I?

ASH Because it's amazing?

IVY How?

ASH You can order what you want, you don't have to talk about boring shit or hear about the other person's day at work or whatever the fuck, you can just enjoy your food or your drink or your book or a podcast, people watch, listen to the next table's conversation, I dunno just be quiet and no one is / there to

IVY Okay well if it's so great why are you asking me to join you?

Beat.

ASH *downs her coffee. It's hot.*

ASH You're right. Thanks for the coffee

ASH *leaves.*

IVY *stands, frozen.* ASH *comes back.*

If you change your mind

ASH *writes her number on a receipt. Leaves.*

IVY *looks at the receipt. Scrunches it up. Puts it in her mouth. Spits it into the bin. Blood spurts out of her.*

IVY I get a pregnancy test just to rule it out

I'm on the pill so it's basically impossible but I just want to rule it out

IVY *does a pregnancy test.*

When ASH *gets home there are more yellow lilies waiting for her. She coughs.*

Heartbeats.

IVY *waits.*

ASH *checks her phone. Kicks some of the flowers.*

Breathes hard in and out.

IVY *picks up the pregnancy test. Stares at it. Puts it down.*

Heartbeats.

Heartbeats.

ASH *puts her hand on the wall to try and steady it.*

IVY *rifles through the bin furiously. Finds the piece of paper with* ASH*'s number on it. Picks up the phone, writes a message. Sends it.*

ASH*'s phone makes a noise. She stares at the screen for a moment. She smiles.*

[*'Freak Like Me' – Sugababes.*]

***

IVY *and* ASH *sit and share a bottle of wine. It's a bit awkward.* IVY *drinks.*

ASH Oh! What's your star sign?

IVY Really?

ASH Yeah go on

IVY I don't believe in all that / shit

ASH Capricorn

Beat.

Knew it

IVY How did you / know that?

ASH Magic

IVY I must have told you my birthday or something

ASH Nope you're just quite a classic Capricorn

IVY Whatever, it's all crap anyway

ASH Sure

IVY What's yours?

ASH Scorpio

IVY Okay, so what does that mean?

ASH It means I'm sexy and mysterious

IVY *drinks.*

IVY Any flaws?

ASH No

IVY No

ASH What's your boyfriend doing tonight then?

IVY Just at home

ASH He didn't wanna join?

IVY I didn't ask him

ASH Why?

IVY Do you wanna text him and invite him?

ASH ? No

IVY Okay

ASH Are you alright?

IVY Fine, I'm really very fine

IVY *drinks.*

Anyway sorry to interrupt your solo drink

ASH It's fine all my drinks are solo drinks. Except when they're not

IVY *drinks.*

Are you sure you're / alright?

IVY Yeah why do you keep asking?

ASH Do you actually want to be here?

IVY Yes I wouldn't have messaged you if I didn't want to be here

ASH You seem really, / like

IVY What?

ASH Wound up, on / edge

IVY Well I'm sorry that must be unbearable to be around

ASH Jesus Christ

IVY drinks. ASH watches.

IVY Look should I just go

ASH What?

IVY This isn't – this is just awkward isn't it, it's just, I'm / just

ASH Fine okay

IVY This was a mistake I mean we barely know each other

ASH If you want to go then go

IVY Why did you ask me anyway like don't you have any friends?

ASH That's a bit / mean

IVY I just don't understand why you want to go to the pub with / me

ASH Well neither do I at the moment because you're acting like a complete dickhead!!

IVY Wow

ASH Sitting there with a face like a slapped arse – what's your problem? I asked you because I like you, because I enjoy talking to you even though you're fucking uptight and judgemental and / ANNOYING to be honest

IVY Well / thanks

ASH AND you interrupt!! It's a really bad habit to interrupt. Like did no one ever teach you when to speak?

IVY wants to interrupt. Instead she drinks.

But for some reason I keep coming back to your stupid fucking overpriced coffee shop, filling out that stupid fucking loyalty card, because I don't actually have any friends at the moment and respectfully it seems like you don't either so. Stay, or go home. I don't care which.

ASH *drinks.*

[*'Wie Die Sonne' – Bal Paré.*] *They drink more.*

They dance – sometimes apart, sometimes together. They dance like they are hungry.

***

The night ends.

They are laughing.

ASH Right I'm gonna get some chips and maybe a kebab

IVY Oh my god I could fucking devour a kebab right / now

ASH DEVOUR

IVY I could fucking DECIMATE a / kebab

ASH I am gonna eat the kebab with like... my entire body

IVY My soul

ASH The kebab is gonna become a part of me

IVY Forever

ASH Where's open?

IVY There's a place at the end of the road

Kebabs appear. They eat.

ASH This was fun

IVY Yeah

ASH We should do it again

IVY Yeah

ASH *looks at* IVY.

What?

ASH Nothing

IVY Have I got sauce on my face?

ASH No

Beat.

I want to kiss you
But I won't because you have a boyfriend

IVY You're drunk

ASH I think you want to kiss me as well

Blood spurts out of IVY.

What does it mean when you do that? Is it when you tell a lie?

IVY Huh?

ASH The blood

IVY What blood?

ASH All the blood

IVY I don't know what you / mean

ASH I don't care. About it

Freaked me out at first but it's obviously just a part of you
Just looks painful
Is it painful?

Heartbeats.

[*'You Belong to Me' – Helen Foster and the Rovers.*]

***

IVY The waiting room has plastic leaflet holders attached to the pillars
There's a mother and daughter sat opposite me
Daughter looks about sixteen, dressed in black school uniform, glued to her phone
Doesn't make eye contact with anyone
Her mum gives me a small smile then lowers her eyes
I pick up one of the leaflets and pretend to read it

ASH, *on the phone, surrounded by yellow lilies.*

ASH No, I haven't actually seen him – well, I think
I actually did once on the Tube but I can't be sure –

…No
…
No but –
…
He hasn't threatened me but he is harassing me.
Well he is calling me all the time he is texting me he is sending me flowers. Like I am drowning in his fucking flowers –
No I don't find it romantic actually

Coughs. Retches at the smell.

…No.
Because I want to keep the proof I'm not about to get rid of the proof I'm not an idiot –

IVY Pill version is easier but also feels drawn out and painful and I'm on a pill already to avoid this particular situation and it didn't work so
I'd rather just get it done make sure it's all out, so
I opt for a surgical abortion and light sedation
The clinician tells me I'll need someone to drive me home
I tell her I can just get an Uber and she smiles at me with a hint of rehearsed pity, tells me I can't go under sedation without a chaperone, so I tell her fine I'll bring one
I'll figure it out later
She books me in for an appointment on Saturday at a different clinic as there's no availability here for a few weeks
Oh – and you should know, she says as I'm almost out the door – that Saturday is when the protesters come.
So just be –
Prepared for that –
I say perfect, can't wait

ASH There must be something you can do

…

So basically you have to wait until he murders me and then you can do something about it? Great. Well I'll call you when I'm dead.

ASH *hangs up.*

[*'Paint it Black' – Rolling Stones.*] *Stares at the flowers.*

Heartbeats.

Heartbeats.

Heartbeats.

ASH *goes over to the wall. Tries to pull at the wallpaper. It won't move. She tries again. She really pulls at it. She is determined.*

She manages to reveal a tiny bit of what's behind – the glimmer of a heart.

IVY *screams.*

ASH *staggers back.*

Trips on the flowers. Kicks them.

Goes back over to the wall, smooths the crease where she tried to rip.

Presses her cheek against it.

My daydreams are just her now

She is in every corner of my brain just waiting
Sometimes I wake up in the night and think I can hear someone in my room
My pile of clothes morphs into the shape of a man, the shape of Cas, looming in the corner
I close my eyes
Put my hand against the wall
And think about what it would be like to press my lips on that bit just under her ear –

IVY *sighs.*

***

A slab of beef.

IVY Again

CAS Steaks!!

IVY I don't *eat / meat*

CAS They're *steaks*, Ivy

IVY Max won't even be able to eat them he's away working they'll just go to / waste

CAS Oh Maxy isn't here?

IVY No

CAS Oh damn

IVY Just your sister I'm afraid!

CAS Never mind

IVY You said you had something to tell me?

CAS Oh yeah the plot thickens

IVY ?

CAS She's dating girls now

IVY How do you know / that

CAS A friend saw her at a dyke club / night

IVY You can't say / that word

CAS Err
It's in the name of the club night actually so I can / say it

IVY Well whatever but if she's a lesbian it explains why she might have not wanted to / get married?

CAS Why the lying?

IVY Sure

CAS We could've made it work.

IVY What do you mean?

CAS Just like have threesomes or something

IVY I don't think that's how it works

CAS Ooooh how does it work then? You'd know

I haven't forgotten your thing with – what was her name?

IVY *walks into the kitchen. Stares at the steaks.*

Beat.

Can you bring some crisps in?
And a beer
Cold beer

IVY *picks up a steak. Pulls off a bit of meat and eats it.*

What was her name… Argh, I can't remember. Fuck. It's on the tip of my tongue.

Emma? Ella? Something like that? Just remember reading it in your diary, so funny. You were so mad, it was so funny.

You'd written a poem or something –

Laughs.

IVY *pulls off another bit of meat. Eats it.*

Do you remember?

That fucking poem was so shit, my god.

Ivy

That's not even the last of it

There's something else

Ivy
Ivy!

IVY *licks the blood off her hands.*

[*'Smalltown Boy' – Bronski Beat.*] ASH *clears up the flowers.*

***

IVY *changes clothes. Puts make-up on.*

ASH and IVY share chips.

IVY You seem on edge this time

ASH Just had a weird day

Beat.

I didn't know if you'd want to meet up again after what I / said

IVY Just forget about it

ASH If that's what you / want

IVY Why was your day weird?

ASH Dunno

IVY You dunno?

ASH It doesn't matter

IVY Just tell me

ASH Why?

IVY Cos telling people things is sometimes good

ASH So profound, can I get that on a tote bag?

IVY Don't be annoying

ASH What do you want from / me?

IVY We always have to have a little row at the beginning don't we, before we can relax

ASH I don't have to tell you / anything

IVY You do. That's what friends do

ASH Friends

IVY Are we not friends?

Beat.

ASH My ex is hassling me

IVY How so

ASH Ringing, texting. He keeps sending me / flowers

IVY Block his number

ASH Genius wow thank you I never thought of / that

IVY Well how is he calling you / then

ASH Just rings from a different one

IVY He has multiple phones?!

ASH I guess

IVY Psycho

ASH Yeah. Today in a voicemail he started commenting on the colours of the walls in my bedroom. And it's weird because he's never been there. So now I keep thinking in the middle of the night that he's in my flat. Or in my room.

Beat.

Anyway it's just my mind playing / tricks

IVY Was he always like this?

ASH No

IVY No red flags?

ASH Not that I noticed

IVY Why did you break up

ASH Loads of reasons

IVY Like

ASH Just loads of reasons

IVY But what reasons

ASH Why do you want to know?

IVY My god have you got a stone I can try and get blood out of it would be less painful than / this

ASH Fuck's sake, I don't know. I can't articulate it all there's so much, it's like a whole – lore, mythology

IVY Mythology!

ASH Yeah

IVY Tell me one bad thing about him

Beat.

ASH He thought that everything was his. Like it was all there for the taking, for his taking. People weren't real they were just bits of food he'd play with. He'd go through my things all the time like my phone, my work / stuff

IVY God

ASH My diary

IVY What was good about him?

ASH He made me laugh. Until he didn't

I didn't handle our break-up very well though

IVY Doesn't seem like he did either

ASH*'s phone rings.*

ASH *God

IVY *Is that him?!

ASH No caller ID so probably / yeah

IVY Want me to answer it? Tell him to go fuck himself

ASH Definitely / not

IVY *reaches for the phone.* ASH *pulls it away.*

IVY Gimme

ASH No it won't help / anything

IVY It might I can be quite scary

ASH I don't think anything will scare him

IVY Are you scared?

ASH No.

Beat.

IVY I have a sofa you can sleep on

ASH No thanks

IVY Why?

ASH I don't think it's a good idea.

IVY It's a better idea than you getting murdered

ASH Cheers

IVY Max is away. The sofa is comfy. Take it or leave it.

***

IVY *gets ready for bed.* ASH *does the same.*

A sleeping bag. IVY *throws it to* ASH, *who catches it, or doesn't.*

ASH Thanks

IVY Do you need anything?

ASH No

IVY You sure

ASH Yeah

IVY Just help yourself to / whatever

ASH Thanks

IVY I'll just be upstairs

ASH Sleep well

IVY You too, sleep well

IVY *leaves.*

IVY *comes back.*

ASH Are you okay?

IVY Yeah sorry, night

IVY *leaves.*

IVY *comes back.*

They watch each other for a moment.

I don't know how to do this

ASH Do / what?

IVY I don't know how to – be. I don't know how to be

ASH Just be yourself

IVY I hate it when people say that because I don't know what it means

ASH Okay

Pause.

Okay

What do you want right now?

IVY In what / sense?

ASH Come on. Ivy. Right now. What do you want right now

In this moment

In this second

Beat.

Do you want me to kiss you?

IVY Yes

Beat.

ASH Are you sure?

IVY Yes

ASH *kisses* IVY.

[*'Maps' – Yeah Yeah Yeahs.*] *They have sex.*

It feels so normal, like putting on a shoe that fits. Like coming to a table filled with food and knowing it's all for you if you want it. She's so careful. She asks throughout, is this okay, is this okay? Do you like this? Do you want this? Can I do this? I nod, I say yes. I say yes. Yes. Yes.

ASH She holds back at first, shy – the shyest I've seen her but then it's like something clicks into place. Then she is this beautiful thing in front of me, on top of me, under me, beside me. She is so alive. She asks me how does this feel? I don't know how to answer. Words don't feel adequate. I say so good. So good. So good –

***

A gift.

IVY What for?

MAX Just for being you

IVY Oh

Thank you

MAX I feel guilty being away all the time!

IVY You don't have to feel guilty

MAX No but I know you hate being on your own

IVY I don't mind it so much these days

MAX I'm gonna be late a lot this week, then I'll probably go up there at the weekend just to make sure everything's okay for the Monday. I know it's crap but it'll be over / soon

IVY It's fine really

MAX Can't wait for all of this to just be done!

IVY You're doing great. I'm proud of you

MAX We should book a trip for after

IVY Yeah

MAX Amsterdam maybe? Or Barcelona! Haha. Too soon / maybe

IVY So you're away the whole weekend?

MAX Yeah sadly

IVY Okay

MAX How's Cas?

IVY Fine

MAX Fine?

IVY Well, not fine. Just the usual

MAX Did he stay over?

IVY Huh?

The sleeping bag.

Oh, no. Yeah, I, sorry. That wasn't Cas, a friend stayed

MAX Who?

IVY Friend from work

MAX Ah

IVY She's having a hard time

MAX Boyfriend trouble?

IVY Ex-boyfriend, yes

MAX Maybe you should introduce her to Cas, might take his mind off / whats-her-face

IVY I don't think / so

MAX On second thoughts with all due respect I would not inflict your brother on anyone

IVY She's gay anyway so I don't think she'd be interested

MAX Oh nice! Cool

Beat.

Do you think she fancies you?

IVY What because she's gay and I'm a woman?

MAX Yeah and you're hot

IVY No.

MAX Well just watch out

IVY 'Watch out'?

MAX She might be grooming you

IVY Grooming me?

MAX I'm joking

IVY She's gay she's not a paedophile

MAX I'm joking!!

IVY And if she was I wouldn't really be in danger / would I?

MAX Do you fancy her a bit babe?

IVY No why are you even / asking

MAX I'm just teasing you it's so easy

IVY Yeah no, you're right. I do fancy her. We fucked in the living room three times last night, actually. Just slightly to the left of where you're standing now. I got the sleeping bag out but we didn't even open it. I can still feel her on my skin. We barely slept. I'm exhausted.

MAX Haha, okay fair enough. Good one

IVY *goes into the kitchen.*

Wanna get started on dinner while you're in there? I picked up some burgers, a veggie one for you as well
Wait – did you even open your present?? Ivy?

***

ASH You didn't say that

IVY I did

ASH Jesus

IVY Cruel of me

ASH When's he back?

IVY Late

ASH I've never been the other woman before

IVY How you finding it?

ASH Like fifty per cent hate myself, fifty per cent find it really hot

IVY Yeah

Beat.

ASH Maybe actually if I'm totally honest thirty per cent hate myself seventy per cent find it / really hot

IVY Yeah

ASH Do you feel bad?

IVY Maybe

I can't tell

I think I'm blocking it out

Like I've put it in a compartment and this –

We. We don't touch it.

ASH You look so good.

Beat.

I haven't stopped thinking about you all day

IVY I need you I am breathless with it

ASH Can I take your clothes off?

IVY Yes

ASH Can I –

IVY I need you to do it like you did the other night –

ASH Yeah?

IVY I need you to make me –

ASH Make you what?

IVY I –

They have sex.

There are yellow flowers everywhere. They are getting more and more impossible to ignore. ASH *keeps tripping on them, stumbling.*

***

[*'Crying Lightning' – Arctic Monkeys.*]

ASH You should come to mine next time

IVY Yours is dangerous

ASH I mean I have to live there

IVY I thought you didn't mind coming here

ASH I don't. It just might be nice for my bed sheets to smell of you sometimes. And might be nice to fuck in a bed and not on the floor, even though there is some charm in that

IVY Yeah I think I have carpet burn on / my thigh

ASH Your thigh yes you do

IVY Sore

ASH Come to mine. Next time

IVY *'s phone rings.*

Beat.

Max?

IVY My brother

ASH Answer it

IVY I haven't got the energy

ASH Okay

IVY Are you hungry?

ASH Yeah

IVY *goes into the kitchen.* ASH *wanders around the room.*

He's handsome

IVY Who

ASH Max

IVY Oh

ASH This is him right? On a boat

IVY Yeah

ASH He's so like

Jocky –

She sees another photo. She is about to move on – then she stops.

[I've seen this photo before.]

Is this you?

IVY Huh

ASH This photo

IVY Well which one cos there's a few

ASH [Why have I seen this photo before?]

IVY Ash?

ASH You – looks like you, but little – and a boy playing with a ball

IVY Oh yeah that's me and my brother!

Speak of the devil he's ringing me again. One sec Cas I can't talk right now I'll ring you back okay I'm at work

ASH *inhales.*

I dunno maybe tomorrow?

Okay

Well he's away anyway so.

Okay bye

Beat.

Sorry.

He's having a shit time at the moment cos his fucking fiancée left him at the altar can you believe that? He calls me all the time now. I used to not hear from him for months and now it's like more than once a day minimum

I don't really know how to help him

They had this whirlwind romance in Barcelona and got engaged after like six months. We never even met her. It was so crazy like I think I saw one photo of her but I barely remember what she looked like. He was very protective, he didn't want to share her. He's quite – controlling isn't the right word, but. He definitely does like, erm

Being in control.

Like he *needs* to be in control or –

He's very persistent you know he's like a dog with a bone he won't let go easily.

He's been trying to track her down –

Beat. IVY *slows down.*

He found out recently that she's dating women and it's really

He's been

Texting and calling and

Sending flowers.

IVY *is still.*

He's been sending yellow lilies

Because that was

ASH Our wedding bouquet

ASH *runs.*

Piles and piles of yellow lilies.

ASH *is out of breath. She leans against the wall. She punches it.*

IVY *clutches her chest. Blood spurts out of her.*

***

IVY *cleans herself up. Changes clothes.*

She hasn't needed us for a while. She is reluctant to speak to us at first.

IVY Cas keeps trying to call me and I don't pick up so he sends loads of sad texts followed by loads of mean texts
If he ever finds out I think he'll kill me
Take me to his job at the butcher's and slice up the rest of me
Wrap it in paper and sell it for an extortionate price

I don't eat because I'd bought all this stuff for us
For me and Ash to eat over the weekend
I was plucking up the courage to ask her to be my chaperone

I bought all this stuff for us
Milky-white buffalo mozzarella
Focaccia from the bakery that always has queues
Big shiny red tomatoes bursting with juice

Every time I look at it I want to be sick
So I eat nothing

Ash was going to bring desserts
Ash was going to bring something sweet
Ash was going to –

What else can I pull out of myself?
When they terminate my pregnancy can they suck my brain out with it? Flush it down the toilet?
Bury it under the floorboards
Go back to my room
To my childhood room
And put all the rest of myself in the walls
Start again from scratch
Assemble myself how I want

I am aching to start again
To do it all properly

I try calling her

Nothing

Nothing.

Blood spurts out of IVY, *a lot of it. More than there has been before.*

I'm not sure what you wear to an abortion so I put on some loose trousers

I go to leave the house and

Thumping –

MAX Surprise!

IVY Oh hey

MAX Caught an earlier train! You okay?

IVY Yeah just about to go to work

MAX Oh shit I thought you had today off!

IVY Picked up a shift cos I thought you weren't back till tomorrow

MAX Cas has been ringing me, says you're ignoring him what's he done this / time?

IVY He's not done anything I just needed some space

MAX Fair

IVY I'll see you later

IVY *gets her coat on, her bag. She turns. She is almost, almost out –*

MAX Hey why don't I come to the café

IVY That's okay I'll just see / you later

MAX No honestly I fancy one of those bougie bacon sandwiches that cost about a thousand pounds

IVY It'll be really busy, / Saturday

MAX Yeaahhh you can nab me a little seat / babe!

IVY I can't really

MAX Of course you can, you've done it loads of times / before

IVY I can't today okay, I'll see you / later

MAX Fine I'll get one to take away

Beat.

IVY Okay I'm not going to work. I didn't want you to worry but I have an appointment, a GP appointment and I'm late.

MAX On a Saturday? What for?

IVY It's nothing to be worried / about

MAX Okay well let me dump my suitcase I'll come / with you?

IVY No it's okay

MAX What is it why you being weird?

IVY I just have to go I have to go on my own I want to be on my / own

MAX You hate the doctor's

IVY I need to go

MAX Hey talk to / me!

IVY There's nothing

MAX Has Cas upset you? What's he been / saying?

IVY Nothing I just need to *go*

MAX I'm not letting you *go* until you speak to me

IVY You're not *letting me go*?

MAX What is it?

Come on. You're scaring me

IVY [He's huge now, he's got bigger, so tall I'm surprised he got through the door, stony muscles showing through his t-shirt –
I can't think of any excuse, any lie I don't have any left in me –]

***

MAX Fuck!! I thought you were on the pill?

IVY I was / I am

MAX Fuck

Fuck.

Okay.

Wow.

I mean to be honest, most kids are accidents

IVY What?

MAX Like we'll have one *some day* / so?

IVY I don't think we've / discussed that

MAX Guess I don't have weak swimmers after all, fuck you, Cas!!

IVY Max

MAX You know this could be our baby

IVY It's not

MAX It's not?

How do you know?

Beat.

Fuck, how could you not tell me?

IVY Because I. Just want to get rid of it.

MAX Oh

Fine but

I support whatever you want to do but when did you stop talking to me? We should discuss things like this, you can't just escape, can't just close yourself off. It's not just you in this. Like, Jesus Christ it's my baby / too

IVY It isn't a baby it's a bunch of cells

MAX My *bunch of cells* then, *my bunch of / cells*

IVY My *body*

MAX I know it's your body! I'm not a dick why are you making me out to be a dick?

I just thought you'd tell me. You should have told me

IVY Yeah

I'm sorry

I'm really sorry

MAX Let me drive you at least

IVY I don't need you to drive me

MAX Christ, I'm trying to help

IVY I don't need your help

Beat.

MAX I feel like –

Like I've walked into my house and everything seems normal but something is also really fucking wrong like someone is in here pretending to be you. You are like familiar but unfamiliar

I don't know who you are. Who are you?

IVY I'm not sure

MAX I love you. I just want to love you

IVY I have to go

I have to go.

The clinic.

ASH The mob are huge today, bigger than usual
I sit at my desk with a shit coffee and try not to think about her
Try not to think about the weekend we were meant to have
About what it was like to kiss that bit under her ear
About how my life suddenly feels like this big fucking wound bristling with infection and –

IVY I forgot about the protesters and there they all are to greet me
There are about eight of them – mostly women, brandishing shiny banners and gory photos
As I get closer one of them lowers their voice
Asks me if I need to talk, if I've been coerced
I look at her banner which reads:
IF MARY WAS PRO CHOICE THERE WOULD BE NO CHRISTMAS
I slide past her and go through the doors –

They stare at each other.

ASH What the / fuck

IVY Sure

ASH Ivy

IVY Hello

ASH Have you followed me here?

IVY Don't flatter yourself

ASH So you're here for an abortion?

IVY No I'm here for lunch. What's the soup special?

ASH Jesus

ASH *slides a clipboard over to* IVY.

Fill this out

IVY Cheers

IVY *starts filling out the form. They speak in low voices.*

ASH Why didn't you tell me?

IVY Why have you ignored me for days?

ASH Keep your voice down.

IVY Oh fuck off

ASH Is Max with you

IVY *looks around, looks in her bag.*

IVY Doesn't look like it does / it?

ASH Ivy stop

IVY Stop what

ASH Is he coming to get you?

IVY No

ASH How are you getting back?

IVY I'll get a fucking cab

ASH You need a chaperone

IVY Well maybe I should call my brother, how about that?

ASH Ivy.

IVY Why don't you ring him you've got his / number

ASH IVY.

Beat.

The reception telephone rings. ASH *picks up.*

Hi

Yep she's here

(*To* IVY.) They've said you can go in now

IVY *hesitates.*

It'll be okay. You won't even know it's happening

***

IVY *has an abortion.*

IVY They're very nice

Gentle smiles and soft eyes
Gentle eyes and soft smiles
I take my trousers off and lie down
Count to three

They inject me with something

One, two –

I vaguely remember tissue-paper underwear
The lights

Blue masks

I wake up feeling elated and hungry

There is a biscuit and a cardboard sick bowl next to me

I look around at the other people in the room and wonder why they aren't eating their biscuits

IVY *shoves a biscuit in her mouth.*

Maybe I could ask for their biscuits?

Probably inappropriate –

***

IVY *leaves the clinic, trips.* ASH *catches her.*

IVY Get / off

ASH I'm taking you back to mine

IVY No thank you

ASH Back to yours, then

IVY No me and Max are done

ASH What?!

IVY Yeah

ASH Well you can't wander the streets you've just had surgery.

IVY Don't care

ASH They're not even supposed to discharge you without a chaperone how / did you

IVY I feel fine, I feel great actually. Empty

IVY *sways* –

ASH I'm taking you back to mine

IVY I don't want to go with you I hate you.

You broke my brother's heart

ASH It's not that / simple

IVY Then you broke *me* open and then you just left

ASH I'm / sorry

IVY Who leaves someone at the fucking altar why didn't you just tell him like a normal / person

ASH Because it was not safe. Because he is not safe.

He is not safe.

You must know that. Ivy. Ivy –

IVY *looks down at the holes in her body. She tries to walk away.*

IVY I feel faint I feel really weird
I feel like I'm not here

Am I here? Am I real?

She falls –

ASH *catches her. Carries her.*
[*'Miss You' – Alabama Shakes.*]

ASH I take her home and put her to bed

IVY *sleeps.*

She sleeps for hours

IVY *stirs.*

Heartbeats.

I go out for painkillers and food
Maybe when I get back I can explain and she'll forgive me
Maybe I can make it alright
Maybe everything will be fine

IVY *stirs.*

Opens her eyes.

Sits up. Looks around.
Heartbeats.

She is frightened at first. She can't believe she is back here. She almost leaves.

Then –

The wall pulses. She stares for a moment. Walks up to it. Puts her hands on it.

Pulls the wallpaper back to reveal her body parts, her beating heart.

She reaches for her heart, pulls it out, holds it up.

Swallows it.

Leaves.

***

ASH *returns with shopping bags.*

Sees the wall. Drops everything.

Looks inside the wall.

Climbs inside the hole in the wall.

It swallows her up.

Then, everything collapses.

ASH *is left in the debris.*

***

ASH *dusts herself off. Cleans up.*

ASH I am honest for what feels like the first time in my life
Really, properly, painfully honest
Like my flesh is raw to the wind
It doesn't make Cas go away at first
It makes things worse for a while
The police are no help but I tell people at work about what's happening
They connect me with a charity and they're great
They support me as much as they can
Till he stops
Which he does, luckily for me
But I think that's mainly because he gets arrested for something else
I heard it was a fight that got out of hand

I reconnect with my mum and dad
They're not happy
My dad is, weirdly, more accepting than my mum
Which I wasn't expecting
So I speak to him occasionally and my mum is getting there

She's warming up

I think, I hope

I'm very lonely
Blisteringly so
Ivy leaves her phone at mine so I have no way of getting in touch after she walks out that day
I search for her
In every crevice of this huge cold brutal city
Sometimes I just choose a stop on the underground and get off and walk

Like a hopeful ghost

She doesn't try and get in touch with me
I don't know what she owes me, whether she owes me anything
I don't know what I owe her either
I try and be a person again
I try and be a happy person
That's a bit harder
I try and find the person I was before I met her
Who'd go to bars alone and not give a fuck what anyone thought
But I can't find her
I don't really know who she was
A year goes by
Then two
I make some really good friends
Friends who I hate sometimes in some moments but never stop loving
I've never had that before
I find a closer version of myself
A balance between who I was before and who I am now
I don't date much
A few minor flirtations with people but nothing important I get a new job
I move flat
Somewhere bigger

I find myself continuously dumbfounded at all the me's that came before this one
I don't know how to reconcile any of it

***

I'm at a gallery
It's November, cold, bright
I've started to enjoy going out on my own again

Cas ruined that for a while but I'm doing it more and more and it's starting to feel peaceful again

There's an exhibition I want to see, this photographer

I'm gallery'd out after about half an hour, embarrassingly
But the good thing about going to galleries on your own is you don't have to feel bad and uncultured when you want to go to the gift shop or café too early
So I go
So I leave.

ASH *leaves.*

A few moments later, IVY *enters through a different entrance. She has a brochure of the exhibition and she drinks a coffee. She's listening to a podcast and enjoying her own company. After a moment, she stops in front of a photograph. Stares at it. Takes her headphones out, as if she can't quite appreciate it with the noise in her ear.*

A few minutes later, ASH *re-enters – confused. She has obviously gone the wrong way.*

She glances at IVY*, almost walks past her. Then she looks back.*

Hesitates.

Heartbeats.

She walks up behind IVY. *Looks ahead at the photo.*

Reaches out to tap her on the shoulder –

Blackout.

End.

A Nick Hern Book

Tender first published in Great Britain as a paperback original in 2024 by Nick Hern Books Limited, The Glasshouse, 49a Goldhawk Road, London W12 8QP in association with Broccoli Arts, Jessie Anand Productions and the Bush Theatre, London

Cover photography by Harry Elletson

Designed and typeset by Nick Hern Books, London
Printed in Great Britain by Mimeo Ltd, Huntingdon, Cambridgeshire PE29 6XX

A CIP catalogue record for this book is available from the British Library

ISBN 978 1 83904 377 2

Woodland CARBON
www.woodlandcarbon.co.uk
NICK HERN BOOKS
Printed on Carbon Captured paper

www.nickhernbooks.co.uk/environmental-policy